THE AFTER PARTY

THE AFTER PARTY

POEMS

Jana Prikryl

TIM
DUGGAN
BOOKS

NEW YORK

Published in the United States by Tim Duggan Books, an imprint of the
Crown Publishing Group, a division of Penguin Random House LLC,
New York.
www.crownpublishing.com

TIM DUGGAN BOOKS is a trademark of Penguin Random House LLC.
TIM DUGGAN BOOKS and the Crown colophon are trademarks of
Penguin Random House LLC.

Selected material previously appeared in *The New Yorker*, *The Paris Review*,
the *London Review of Books*, *Harper's*, *The New York Review of Books*, *The
Nation*, *The Baffler*, the *Literary Review of Canada*, and *The Unprofessionals:
New American Writing from the Paris Review*.

Library of Congress Cataloging-in-Publication Data
Names: Prikryl, Jana, author.
Title: The after party : poems / Jana Prikryl.
Description: New York : Tim Duggan Books, 2016.
Identifiers: LCCN 2015137658 | ISBN 9781101906231 (paperback) |
ISBN 9781101906248 (epub)
Classification: LCC PS3616.R538 A6 2016 | DDC 811/.6—dc23 LC record
available at https://lccn.loc.gov/2015037658

ISBN 978-1-101-90623-1
eBook ISBN 978-1-101-90624-8

Printed in the United States of America

Cover art: Elliott Green's *The Thing Imagines Itself* (detail), 2014
Cover photograph: Michael Fredericks

10 9 8 7 6 5 4 3 2 1

First Edition

for Voyta Prikryl
(1968–1995)

CONTENTS

I.

THE AFTER PARTY

I.

Ontario Gothic

1.

The dwarf maple caught my attention
in an ominous way, its purple,
its deep purple leaves shredded gloves
that gesture "Don't worry, don't worry,"
among floating albino basketballs of hydrangea
among other things the people landscaped
like fake lashes round the top of the eye
that then all summer takes in clouds
and anything else passing over, including
one has to assume
the neutral look
on a passenger's face glancing down from a window seat.

2.

Halfway there he squeezed between the shoulders of the seats
to join his wife and me in back. I need hardly tell you
what a stretch it was, wedging my arm between the driver's seat and door
to steer with the tips of my fingers,
sidewalks in those parts just wide enough for a car.
Why he wanted me to take the wheel
I was too busy not getting us killed
to unravel; there was the traffic, a thing
coming at us with its mouth wide open, and in back
the two of them
whispered in their corner,
taking up very little space,
less than was right,
and then less and less, gasping at the joke he'd set in motion.

Argus, or Fear of Flying

A seagull at home in this valley steps into air
above the river. I'd like to follow
it holding the wind to account while flinging
itself out into it. Remove in reading
and being the music when you listen—
not that you moved back but forward into
remove—saw you off a wall patched with lichen,
consortium of air and electric currents
it'd be difficult to itemize
expressing you across the river.
It deepens like a mind accruing images.

I keep the beat, the tune a repetition,
indifferent its source or whether
rock and roll or country, junkier the more
immense, as with all the airborne arts,
and you keep your distance, convexity
of feeling, and relations of the third person
vis-à-vis a situation.
It's crucial to no more than misplace
claims on what might go down with the pilot's
resourcefulness—it cannot look too
casual—faculties both stirring up
and yielding to motion bestowing lift.

The statues of Hermes littering Europe
with little fins at head and feet don't conjure
the fact articulated through my limbs
when I read about Zeus flying him in
on winged sandals to murder the diligent
freakish strangely beautiful giant

tasked by the jealous wife with guarding
the innocent mistress—you see there's always
demand for aviation—in which the god's
center of gravity over his lofting
feet emerges as something palpable,
autonomous disc near the pelvis
of an ally that's never not mobile.

Pillow

How solitary
and resolute you look in the morning.
A stoic in your cotton sleeve.
Do you dream of walking out

rain or shine
a truffle balanced on your sternum
and passing me on the sidewalk?
Or is that a smile

because you interpret nothing
and statelessness is where you live?
How calmly you indulge my moods.

See you tonight, by the sovereign chartreuse
ceramics at the Met.
Let's hear what you'd do differently.

Tumbler

It was too much
to hope for to
hope we would know
when too much was
too much to hope
for.

New Life

From the fields of a calendar, its snow
packed firmly into squares, I farmed you.
    Following some paperwork you shipped west
    and I flew home economy.
        An interval like summer passed before a van found my house
        and tilted you off the dolly.

Tucked behind hedges and twilight, with a screwdriver
I pried the lid and under
    petals of bubble wrap
    your eyes open,
        blue as an infant's
        and equally foreign.

That your English came back as fast
as it did was more than anyone could've asked.
    You soon made friends
    just as I'd predicted.
        You sleep in the spare room—no closet or chair
        but a window onto something green and unconflicted.

Afternoons were tennis, sandwiches,
and drills recalling the yellow bike, the seven stitches.
    I know it tires you.
    Mustn't overdo it.
        Your memory worked pretty well
        considering the mirror time put to it.

In thinking back you'll try to invent
the future: you see us growing ancient,
   say, twenty-nine, translated
   in dad's shirts and ties.
      It's the past, when brother and sister
      were all footsoles and eyes
         together in a wood as steep as the Tyrol
         that looms up unannounced, always a surprise.

Unrequited

He'd have called to say the sill is overrun
with moss, there's moss on the light fixtures, moss
on his prepositions, when he bends and unfastens
himself from bed, he finds moss on his clothes,
a soft green runway of fuzz in the most
interesting section of his underwear.

I know what you need, the law's wide dry hands
trying to bucket the truth: And nothing but
the small transparent sphere that breaks and fills
the moss's thousand tiny throats. Let's imagine
for a minute he has the soil, is really in it—
Levin moving through the rows with a scythe.
His feeling is metaphor so complete
it's the hum alone on loan from the hive.

A Package Tour

It's not untruc to say that Paní Barvíková was a great-grandmother
or she and three others were great-grandmothers
although they were unknown to one another
and to themselves as great-grandmothers.

Before those four, there were eight. Then sixteen,
and at thirty-two we could charter a bus (with room
for their trunks) and tour the Loire, chateaux already then antique.

It's a costume drama of uncertain date; be not too dogmatic
in your visualization but do picture us
looking fabulous.

These being the days a woman's body's
respected absolutely in its tyrannical seasons
the better to be exploited absolutely.

I called them by their unpronounceable names:
Paní Vejvodová, Paní Frgalová.
Old tapestries of politeness swung substantially between us.

Even the legal rapes that bit them into keeping
secrets from themselves had hit them early enough at least
to yield fat little dividends.

From time to time
one of them would touch my hair or take my arm,
laying a gentle claim.

I saw one whispering into hands cupped
to a window; her words appear
as subtitles in the making-of documentary.

Even the wealthiest, most finely dressed, most widely read
in Romance languages shrank beside the poise of the French,
and so plus ça change.

They were my mothers, all,
but I was their guide,
I hoisted a furled umbrella.

I had my career, it's important to me
to do some work of significance
or do my work conscientiously.

At night the Château de Chenonceau is lit with torches like a cake.
Aristocrats in period dress play their forefathers
in a hedge maze floodlit from below.

Puddles of rouge under the eyes
of also most of the men, perukes and heels impelling them to caper.
Some comic scenes when I mistake a few for great-grandmothers.

You know we've grown close because now
there's something close to rivalry between us. Quietly in clusters
they agree their lives meant something regardless,

regardless of my arrival.
Why did you show us all these things?
What do you bring besides information?

Meanwhile I'd begun to sense, although this sense
was gradual and liable to withdrawing,
that I didn't depend on them to feel entire.

I hated to leave them
I couldn't refrain from saying
in their bad marriages.

And then I was here,
remembering the ovals of their faces
like blank money,

as if this could win me some advantage,
as if it might incline you to be generous.

Benvenuto Tisi's *Vestal Virgin Claudia Quinta Pulling a Boat with the Statue of Cybele*

[*a painting at the Palazzo Barberini in Rome*]

A solid quarter
of it is blotted burnt umber
for the hull, a scripted curve, as if color
bricked over and over
could send a sailboat blowing from the canvas as matter.

Similar:
shipping the goddess from a backwater
then setting her up here.

And I'm the golden retriever.

Eyeballed from behind, female with yellow hair
contending with a hawser.

Manifestly unafraid to show my rear.

"Sip antiquity from my spot on the Tiber!"

Daylight buzzing like an amphitheater.

Not everyone is born to be a master.

He did sketch Michael roosting with his sword
on the grave of the Roman emperor
in perspectival miniature,
echo of the statue in the fore.

More on her later,
all the eunuchs and bees you can muster.

If you had to name the gesture
of the frontman with the beard
and frock of a Church Father
gaping at me from the future,
you could do worse than *basta*—hands perpendicular
to the ground, each white palm a semaphore,
head tilted halfway between concern
and something he won't declare.

To all the girls Bernini loved before
I'd say, caveat emptor.

The deathless ars
longa, vita brevis guys will have me clutch a carved
toy boat but this provincial follower
of Raphael goes for the ocean liner.

Reality's my kind of metaphor.

The heavens circulate with the times on the far
horizon and I don't have anywhere
to be except this unambiguous shore.

Tumbril

You have to hope we
soon exhaust all hope because
you sense one final hope
and maybe the true one
can be hoped for only
after every hope has lost
its head.

The Letters of George Kennan and John Lukacs, Interspersed with Some of My Dreams

You asked me about myself. In May
I remarried, three and a half years
after I had lost my unique wife.

Depression, at least in my case,
has much to do with my physical
and psychic state of the moment.

My words are carved on gravel stones, each about the size
of an oyster, and must be fed in the proper sequence
into a gadget like a water gun.

Those striking lines from John Donne correspond
exactly with something that I read
by Kierkegaard

some time ago: in which he says that Truth
is given to God alone: but what is given to us
is the pursuit of truth.

My gravel words drift slowly through the water
toward a sort of muzzle that spits them out,
and that is how I speak.

For the second time, I am blessed in having found
a charming, warm-hearted, intelligent woman,
sparkling with *esprit*.

In a Pennsylvania town the bedframes are made of iron,
the dolls are still porcelain, and the trolleys
pulled by long lines of white horses in single file.

It is a rainy Sunday morning, and I have asked our guests
to excuse me while I do some writing. I, too,
sense the imminent arrival of great calamities.

I look down and see through my skin
to the infant inside: he grows horns on his head
but my seeing it makes them go away.

The arrival of the letter found me in a state of comparable despair.
Being essentially a healthy person I recover
by indulgence in the little satisfactions of the moment.

My room has a terrace that looks down on steep hillsides
dropping to the sea, like a Bruegel. As I admire the view
a bay horse clops across the road.

This state of mind came in part from personal reasons,
notably the realization of my failure to bring about
a better understanding of nuclear weaponry and Soviet–
   American relations.

The horse chain has broken in several places
and it is my job to hitch a number of white horses
to other white horses.

No one knows what will be left when this process
of disintegration has been halted—
possibly only the Russian heartland.

Deer outside my window in Manhattan,
and woods, and a girl on a horse, and then
snow begins to fall in thick, slow clumps:

this, it seems to me, is what I'd hoped for
so I grab my camera,
intending to send you the picture.

Inverted Poem for the Fluoride Ladies
of Pleasant Valley School

Their uniforms remain
but this is not the place to tell you
the other things I cannot bring to mind.

They stand erect, side by side, and shine
like knowledge.

If I were them, once installed behind a desk
I'd leave my post with some reluctance.

The ladies drove sedans along our valley's
curving roads, each preferring certain bends
it's not worth telling anyone about.

Who remembers where the juice was spat?

They set out rows of cups on two desks shoved
together, each thimble of wax paper
Lite-Brite, expressed from grapes or rubies
or Orange Crush, and we file past, take one,
gargle at our desks where only pencils
ought to be an eternity that wrings
each eye till we're allowed to spit—in what?

What kind of movies did they like to watch?

The ladies who came
and went from class to class with lab coats
buttoned over pencil skirts and mom sweaters:

They flash,
the lasting last formal thing in a face
that flows and thickens.

They come in so many
shapes and arrangements, and as we age
they grow more pronounced, more like ourselves,
or like ourselves quite lost to us.

Despite what I was taught in school
there really is a spectrum of uniqueness
and most teeth partake of a great deal
of uniqueness.

I wish I didn't look at people's teeth
so much.

Ars Poetica

1.

What we are most
easily seduced by must
tell us something
about ourselves, but what
if it tells us only
about everyone else?
If you want to get
to know someone (tweets
the prolific Kelly
Oxford) argue with him,
and I considered
that wisdom, considering
my recent disagreements with you
there reading this.
Let me here drop too
a word on Arthur Conan Doyle's
surrender to the disciples
of Madame Blavatsky,
or some cognate matter
acting as foothold.
Let me be the last,
in other words,
if you can arrange it,
the last of the last
to plead the colorless
autonomy of language
houses a will as acquisitive
as ours, if not more so,
gripped by dreams

of description, unmitigated
description even unto
argument, argument
so humorless it teeters
back into the realm of description
and drops its mask
and spits in every dinner plate.
The last, I said. For who
would call that seduction?

2.

Thinking of Benedict
Cumberbatch and his mind
(stay with me), I resolved
on the importance
of character, specifically
as a function of the celebrity
interview: that it's not his face
propelled him into the skin
of a leading man but
his quips and winning
earnest wish to answer
every question
and be very very nice.
Just so
the novelists will not
hazard any but the finest
manners in their prose, no
they won't, they won't,
they've shown
they won't for two
maybe three generations,
those maestros of exposition,

and that may be what's driven
the poets to this bluff
of severely impartial
impudence.
I was thinking this walking
home in the dark, the too-early
dark of November, shivering,
toward my apartment
on a promontory,
fingers stiff
hauling staples,
wondering if it was the kind
of thing that, were I the second-
last person at a party
with Benedict Cumberbatch,
he'd find worth debating,
call a very good question,
before proposing we spare
each other the embarrassment
of being the last
to leave and leave in unison.
Goodness that shows
every sign of being also
resourceful has always been so
difficult to refuse.

Siblings and Half Siblings

We sisters had the Vondörfer hair,
pink with ripples and electrodes in the right places,
wavy orange stuff environing our faces.

We were lucky with our looks—decked
in matter—like everyone on earth.
That they divorced us prior to my birth

and raised me in a land of unicorns
and you in the Bloc, eating cabbage
and drinking Becherovka, now seems tolerable baggage

for these waves, which brandish so. Yet just how
the old guys did it seems not too wide of.
I dare you ask how he took brother aside

between one alp and another on that
Austrian postcard and punted:
Where would you like to grow up?

Father had muscle enough to ask such a thing
of his one son and son had the stiff upper
to say: Yes, run me away from mother

and sister. Did his yellow hair luff
in a gust as he stood there
turning the question around in his mouth?

Did he stare and pocket his fists?
He was twelve, it was obvious.
He granted going west,

possessing what he'd soon get more of, belief,
a style of ampleness—not without doubt
but without the files of teeth

that make food of us from inside.
Thanks to that one's nerve
the four of us boarded an overnight

and this is English, more or less.
But those were other times.
To marry and remarry and reproduce

bent you to the general disease; exeunt with care
and scrapes. We, sister, have our degrees
of pleasure and our tantrums when they fail to please.

Tombolo

To keep them safe in time
of war we evacuated our hopes
to this island made of sand
dredged from the ocean floor thanks
to the moon's land grabs and
remain calm if the ocean floor
under sway of the same moon
collects itself like an orator, forming
ways to talk about our island
until it quarantines no hope anymore,
young foreigners walking in and out
placing carnations and each one removing
a small stone.

Stanley Cavell Pauses on the Aventine

At the side of the slope where all those waves
of Romans neglected to put much else,
a lane goes down to the Tiber between
two sweating walls, streetlamps, views of the city's
one monument not scuffed ochre—columns bride-
white, ponced with wings, the bronze quills
a bylaw from touching behind each back.
If I say this in the tone of a photograph
will it inject you with the feeling
I felt in that place? Now I'm released
from the wish to euthanize this feeling
by means of knowing it's felt by everyone.
Unworkable as "at no time in the history
of photography could you have learned photography
in part by photographing photographs." Maybe not
but if you wrote descriptions like photographs
couldn't you deepen as a painter who
through most of the history of painting
learns to paint by copying paintings?
From here you see not the square itself
but the campanile locating it where
a replica of Marcus Aurelius's bronze
reminds you of his sentences, so measured
and reliable, with the occasional self-
recrimination in the text you're helpless
to read as anything but a Polaroid of his skin.
The lane is quiet and some people reside
in two blue tarps staked to the slope that's piled
against a wall, cultivating legumes
and herbs between the domes of thistle.
An American said he came here once

at sunrise to film a scene and a fiftyish woman
strided out, shrieked the dollar's rape of Italy
on the British model, hexed art-school types, cried
Lampedusa, saints' rites, a curse on modest designs
and immodest designs. He introduced himself
as mildly as I've known him to say anything
and she said her name was Eleanor.

To Tell of Bodies Changed

Having desired little
more than the

arrival of the little more
that arrives,

outside our window a cypress
of model proportions.
Its patience seems to widen
the nights we sleep in Rome.

Warm flags draw a tortoise,
it scrapes too near.
Our friends hurry over when they hear,
exclaiming over its mute
resolute
distinctness and helpless slow efforts to flee.

Density pours into swallows and shadows:
spilled with abandon each morning,
begins then the slow work
of receding.

The joints announce their new allegiances.
Metaphors swarm the surfaces of things.

Night broken into, it's the sub rosa
singling out
I ought to have expected
from Fra Angelico's small panel
among others,

the souped-up full-spectrum wings
combined with a mood of reverent submission
in both figures
warning of experience
yet to come.

Starting now she'll reason with herself
deliberately
(imagine bulbs expecting stars
for effort!), aware of being always overheard,
subject to unprecedented measures
of integrity, like an author.

While a substance of landscape, mineral,
leaches into blood vessels
quietly steadily, meaning in this case
nothing is damaged;
extravagance of umbrella pines
propping their fingers under the bonus horizons
of the hills, redundancies
boosting the city's resemblance to itself.

A painter once squared himself against a difficult question
and said no one could just create
a landscape,
but isn't it true
that expectation builds a neighborhood
and there is nowhere else that you can live.

It was possession, turns out, by a force whose intention
touched the first body alone, a body changed
again precisely to its own form,
a very special intention.

Alloyed
discretion, the grit of a damp trowel
explores my mouth, at leisure
determining
the candor that cavity
is good for.

Ode/Our Hospitality

"No begging."
—Buster Keaton

You who found none of your codirectors sufficiently serious, the scene
in need of reshooting,
the Civil War, plantation mood, the trouble was to lay the keel
down near enough to fact
to send those uncommon orders of feeling from your eyes to none but ours
when a gun went off at dinner,

I mean a popped cork, and you unmurdered, alive in the sense that
projectors stutter
stern-black pages to light you into motion for our no less than
physical pleasure

Your glance like an open hand, your glutes, your hurricane tending by its own
momentum to the next exposure
of an inner mechanism, whose parody sinks its point into the mark to such
a depth it spreads
to illumine the entire body and every other body and the number of you
in all the parts
seem a sort of human finale, if not the very last absolutely necessary
movie, then the first and last

We'll sit you in a chair and grant you days of banqueting in safety
to think of new material

A Place as Good as Any

Outside the funeral of the politician who died young
I waited for you. Rolled in my hand like a baton

were tissues from the mourners inside
that I was meant to throw away,

a few with your scribbled notes to me.
How they'd found me in that crowd I couldn't say,

or if the bottle blond was your wife
or whether I had a husband.

We sat near enough to barter
knives and forks—the scraps of dinner theater.

The blond was climbing into your lap,
playing with the buttons on your jacket.

Then all of us rose and circulated, more like a whirlpool
than musical chairs. You on the far side of the banquet.

That's when you wrote me those notes, one by one,
that stiffened into typescript in my hand.

At times I glanced toward your place
and we locked eyes like opponents in chess.

Your hair was still so thick and dark
I didn't worry if I looked older.

When I waited for you outside, clutching the tissues
and pulling up tufts of grass, your friend's shoulder

presented itself. He said you lived in this town
and couldn't be caught leaving with me.

I nodded, ducking back into the paneled saloon
where he'd blacked out and was sprawled across linoleum.

He agreed to drive me to the film festival.
You'd be there in the dark with strange women and men,

absorbed in pictures more honest than these
if I ever found you again.

Tumblehome

We had
to kill our
hope and heave it
over the side and drift
alone into the flat gray morning
without sail, finding it the only way
to proceed at all considering the threat
of ambush by a hopelessness we might
have failed to anticipate, which in anticipation
was intolerable and it is not too
much to say that habit of prudence
is the reason why we are still
here.

The Tempest

Parked magenta Lumina,
aluminum awning, wool shoulders
of a coat shrugged on to run across the street

for milk await
the formalwear of snow,
remote from adjectives.

The sky won't stoop to it so much
anymore, the banks of cloud
unhitch and crumble down.

On our way to the party we stopped at a bar,
three girls in the din of a Friday night
to warm up and find ourselves late.

It's not just the coming-into-being of the air
but the silence and smell, coldly
suggestive, of ozone meeting earth.

Such a gigantic abstraction withheld
makes a person feel
more creaturely than is proper.

You very nearly
come out and tell me
what it is you came here for.

In that peopled brown-lit place I find
I don't want to talk to anyone much
and wait like a child while the two others talk.

This Tunis sir was Carthage,
comes the voice of a man,
sincere,

who circles to his meaning despite how many
push him off it, a patient man,
I assure you Carthage.

One day it returns, half an hour
the motes drift close
with the care of airplanes flying low over the city.

For experience shows that timing one's arrival
at a party is easier to do
in the company of others.

Is not sir my doublet as fresh as the first day I wore it?
A doublet, a doublet. In my edition the notes
concur with the scoundrels,

Tunis and Carthage were close
but not the same city.
Also you learn the reasons for your amusement,

if that's what it is, when they mock the mention
of Dido, have not been explained.
How came that widow in?

What if he had said "widower Aeneas" too?
It's funny to use your imagination
because it's true.

And tears of a lackey,
the touch of a known hand,
an ordinary consolation

undoes me. I pause for them to move
from higher to lower regions of the sky
before proceeding down the sidewalk.

Understudy

1.

The land's forever making noise
of rise and fall, the grand parabola.

But must it always paraphrase?
The moon can't blink its shining cornea

toward the setting sun. It's in the line
of fire, it's hit by little sparks.

And they, neutrinos rich and bored, will pay
a kiss for a kiss for—*POMPEII*:

your talk of exes going nuclear, your video
countdown to the end of a casino—

maybe down the crescent of the bay
above the belt of Verrazzano.

A second city then will crack up
beside the one in need of backup

and no harm done, no need to be on
a packet to pave old Île d'Orléans.

2.

The city's an amphora, broken-dishy.
The bits were nicked to model demolition.
Stacked and drowning, stacked and drowning.
The qui vive is the salt spray owning
knowing bunkers defunct since Vichy.

It Doesn't Work Out as I Read Roland Barthes's *Mourning Diary* and *Camera Lucida*

A little girl as she was in his childhood now
become a grandmother, Mavra, who simply
concerns herself with the family she loves,

without raising any
problem of *appearance*,
of sanctity, of the Church, etc.

    Lady in the tall forehead
    beating your winglike
    eyelids down, feel free, don't hesitate, etc.

She never employs a meta-language,
a pose, a deliberate
image. That's what "Sanctity" is.

    The climate around us encourages
    misunderstandings that are not,
    we both know, misunderstandings.

O the paradox:
I, so "intellectual"
(which I defend).

    But rather rhapsodies
    of communication
    whose highways roar with words

all the same year and make,
roaring in four directions.
There are no accidents.

She offers me
in the highest degree
her nonlanguage.

Smiling is an exercise,
great convoys
crossing the plain.

And finally her expression,
which distinguished her, like Good
from Evil, from the hysterical little girl.

Sun flashes its whitening teeth
on every windshield
advancing in one long code.

From the simpering doll who plays
at being a grown-up. The frivolous
insignificance of language,

the suspension of images
must be the very space
of love, its music.

We have this field, we know
our place, where each says I'd put
nothing past you.

Genealogy

Those barnlike buildings dressed in pastel
pajamas patterned in stucco dingbats,
florals, orchard fruit, faces that weathered
honest crops of burghers without winning
a curator's interest, roofs deep skullcaps
with gables lopped, where stiff planes of shingles
bestow on them the primordial air
of foreheads sublet to hairdos

still shrug at the castle, the whites of whose
fenestrations blink a light now speakable,
and at a loss to drop the slightest hints

regarding the forms of their diligence
suffer apartment blocks, jungle gyms to be
as free in their approach as those who fly

coach to look at them for a few minutes.

Titoism

We shall Tito on the brink, we shall
Tito on the edge, we shall watch our
hopes Tito in the balance, we shall never
give up, we shall never surrender, being what
we are will mean an amniotic swaying from
one foot to the other, the childish motion
moving our parents to fight the fight so
forty years from now they kiss at last
and we are free.

A Motion in Action

An animal again in the mint-green stall, one of five, and for once
unembarrassed to be
doing my business here, very near another person and quite
near the upholstered cubicle
where a mechanical pencil has its way with me
half my waking life.

From the pomp of this circumstance such accuracy scatters
that failing
to study it would be reckless spending yet all my ingenuity—

not just finding a way to sit ten minutes in the eighteenth-
century church
at lunchtime, white within and cool/hot as a nun,
eighteenth-century
bottle glass silently intact in all the windows, and two angels
carved above the sanctuary,

each with its wings extended like a balance pole and balancing
on a small wheel like a piece
of rotelle pasta, but also every moment of the day as if I were one

of those angels as unblinking as they are unseeing
meticulously collecting my attention not so much inside myself
as folded in and in, into itself, a muscled gymnastic laboring
to remain intact on the rotelle and outpace the extension
of any perspective, however inward and tenebrous, which would be
exterior to the attention, therefore arduous—all my ingenuity

is spent like this,
or almost all, no doubt that's an exaggeration. It is the coil's
imperative

to render
the little flash across the landscape conserved on weekends
at home, openings
of substance between the islands of the diagram that stop
their lips
precisely when I'm rich, alone with it and free to look at it.

Crackers

Sometimes—sometimes we do not go so good
together. We go to school and other
times we change. I, to shake the clods, ignore
the phone; you can't connect; resulting mood
is glum. What you have to say won't bother
waiting for an occupied—it rings more and more

till I pick up. What's up at home?
and similar caulk to plug us from the sea
exchange—what time we woke, who made the tea—
till we run out of talk. Then hold the phone

without a word, just a rustling soothing
box of crackers voice themself, and on
the final crisp you sigh the line has gone
to sleep, and hadn't we best be moving?

New York New York

Between two chairs
    that say so little
        for themselves

sitting one another out
    either side
        the East River

like an actor seated
    backwards, legs
        astride the chair

what meets me then
    walking one island
        or other

and in this scenario
    I am half
        the actor

stage and screen
    whose moves
        wow the well read

what meets me then
    old flame
        sufficiency

Monologue for Two Voices

There are few things in the world more beautiful
than a university, the president in 1963
continues saying to me now.
I was doing a bunch of different things
but that voice was irresistible.
The strangers slumped against me on the train
who sleep like horses, upright and out
to pasture, they are that
exhausted, would say the same.
A small nation loves its great men
jealously. The nation learns
to be a molecular scientist,
a lifestyle of always resuming
precisely where another left off
and adding on what you can spare of yours.
A water flowing through different lands,
abundant and continuous while observing
its banks and the farms on either side,
carrying certain men there and back
with time to compose accounts of how it was,
has not historically been my problem.
Where there's less to own you have
to own it a lot more
than those who have more own theirs.
It's understandable.
As a child I got the flu each time
a special day would beckon.
So childhood was one long influenza
and I made reparations to myself in the form
of a terrible sympathy with each new fact
that could be planted in the mind.

I've never again known such intimacy.
Except what I keep to myself when a man
taught at American University
writes my mother tongue more fluently than I can.
Don't let me interrupt you
already in the door stating his business the person
from elsewhere is supposed
to mean disaster up until
disaster flavors the coolness of the room
and unfolds its own topography
of darker and lighter shades. It's later
you see the little jerks
of youth, the little thrills, were ancient
signals pouring in like ocean waves
with their gratifying sound of applause,
washing over you from some primitive source,
while the first signs of age, which after
a few decades of youth arrive like carnivals
to vary a long holiday by the seaside,
these changes in their novelty will feel
like youth. For a while you welcome them
with interest and in a kind of innocence.
Will monotony ever again
resemble itself?
There must be a formula anyone could use
to tell how many more times I'll need
to feel so unprepared.

Timepiece

Do not lose hope.
We found new hope.
There is no hope.
You have to hope.
It's my last hope.
There's always hope.
It grows on trees.

The Moth

"New research suggests that butterflies
and moths come with mental baggage
. . . left over from their lives as larvae."
—*Science*

He'd like to be at one with his new self
but memories sit in him like eyes.

Sometimes scent implies an unheard-of
idea and he's off
but it's just another of the given forms.

You'd think flight would be decent redress,
the power to sift himself through air
and leave each thought in its old place,
where hard feelings also could be left.

He shrugs and the wings
quiver with great precision,
nature will have to live with what it's done,
he cannot manage even resignation
without a show of grace.

Landscaping

You pulled up the lawn like a carpet,
positioned a new one as you went. They forced it

upon you when the seasons changed.
At the social up the hill I was trying to enjoy champagne.

Where the grass threw its skirt over the ravine
it framed your head and shoulders, a boy by Chardin

at work, unposed. You had crooked teeth
and straw-colored hair, so that was half

the details right. Later I fled the wicker affair
and joined you on the slope. We spoke the words

that crowd in at the end of visits. You detailed
how you coil up the turf and fetch it away

like one regifting a responsibility.

Geodes of the Western Hemisphere

The earth has feelings
some killed others in its mud and it has lots of mud

The earth builds a scrapyard, a sequence of them to tell
of this, a seam on its embalmed glabella future galaxies caress

The earth knows André Breton,
compiles ingenuous personalities in its fevered correspondence

Out of its winding sheet rolodex the earth erodes another name,
your name

Beware, the earth prepares to say one final time, construction
eclipses

It hoped to say nothing further and then was disappointed, its hope
misplaced it knew deep down

Say more,
you say, the earth had hoped you would

Express as little as possible with your furniture, find the little that is
as near to nothing as can be

The monuments unpictured drift up like watermarks through the odor
of the lens

You make things happen all the time, says the earth, take my advice
look the other way

II.

Thirty Thousand Islands

Mr. Dialect pauses on a bluff
twice pink in the spreading lakes,
his suit bespoke
and out of style.

His very mood
an index
of gestures that the artist
oversteps.

Where should he look
for the abiding tinge
that flushes the cheeks
of all these second homes?

Compulsive translator, in time he'll slip
the modesty that's his;
he too
reaches for effects.

And the other one
who is not upside down
in the lake, rippling,
with almost the same intensity

sends regrets.
He wanted to go to some expense
in meeting you,
with care for the adjectives.

*

Mr. Dialect alone
cast a shadow at noon.

He did it by leaning
slightly.

*

It's far from my wish
to identify
with the nameless
on these islands,

he thought.
His eyelashes blond
as his collar, and he mild
in his vanity.

When he could pause
on a chronicled bridge
exciting the guess
of a dozen origins,

why putter here
hard by cottages
very few of which
screen the famous?

It's far from obvious
that I'm sufficiently
personal. For one,
this tie's Hermès.

*

Mr. Dialect is generous
with problems of metaphor.

They are not his problems

but he'll acquiesce
to all of these islands.

*

The Indians announcing cigars
and vacation days
of a vanished clientele,
with sanded surfaces distinct

and eyes fixed
on the far gone,
long after the product stopped selling
and moved to where the money was

stayed on,
fading and slanting
into the small dirt beaches—
they consent to sentinel the place,

they quietly repel
any but the most literal description.
That one they also repel.
And that one.

*

This, we thought, his country.
Mr. Dialect a natural.
Foreign—distinct thereby,
thereby typical.

But with a sadly proud gesture
of refusal
he said, Madam, I never
eat muscatel grapes.

He clears his throat
and shifts it into neutral.
Gives a slow exploratory
draw on the starter.

When it argues,
hauls back from the shoulder
and turns into what passes
there for open water.

*

The boat takes you shopping
for ketchup and cereal.
If the shack at the gas pump
had a decent selection

of reading material,
a man could avoid
buying *Playboy*
just for the articles.

*

Mr. Dialect conserves
like a master tactician
the best of his Parisian shirts:

to the village launderette
hefts a garbage bag.
At the jump from washer

to dryer nets
each one-hundred-percent
remnant in the sack,

shouldering them back
to the houseboat and pats
their sleeves onto wire hangers—

eaves of the *Never Better*
seized by a flock
of pastel bats.

*

My Paris shirts, the famous
dead, hang cuff to cuff
in the hanging locker,
press for a puff
from the hand steamer,
a Tuesday promenade
in Honey Harbour,
the light down to a stub
of ash on the top deck,
its fiberglass warm
and bumpy as the retrospect,
some Rémy, Ritz crackers,
and the usual come-ons
from stars overhead.

*

The sky now kindling
for him alone at five
in the morning,
Mr. Dialect will rise
let's say most days
(there are no others)
with an air of dressing
to breakfast beside
a caramel brunette,
her taste in shoes
unswervingly superb.
It's not among
the things he learns
to tire of such blessings.

*

A set of rocks like mountaintops whose mountainflanks
are plunged in a body of water.

Down in the valleys astronauts
water rhododendron pots,
their faces sealed in mason jars.

To floss their teeth or make some calls
they climb the rungs of a ladder
underwater
and drag themselves over a boulder.

When the voices start confiding their Christian names
as I'm rinsing plates on the *Never*

it's time to haul anchor, wait
in a dive in Parry Sound,
and buy a round
for whoever won't be a stranger.

Should a drink materialize
you didn't order, make eyes
at the girl who didn't send it, as I'd have done.

*

A neighborhood sketchy with white pine,
red pine, white pine, blueberries
small in size and glaucous.

Wrinkles in the gneiss run parallel
as if an island had its uses
at one time, its maneuvers.

An animal tone
to the granite
as it masses and hides in the water.

And trees that lean from the rock
defy photographers. Stoic raconteurs,
parked here just this aeon,

limbs widely down on
the twist investing
every vertical.

*

Where stacked skyscrapers of frozen water carved the pink-complexioned
rock into this feminine shape, he stands
a diagnosis on his face
a smile inclined
at the fury of masters perceiving the privileges of their kind extinct.

*

Somewhere nearby
Mr. D crouches
down a cheekbone of azoic rock,
hornblende granite,
back to the back
of the aluminum boat.

Water sloshing the sides of the boat,
oddly abrasive hollow sound
like buying real estate.

For instance
B578,
a natural harbor to the north
and three inlets to the south like swimming pools,
later named, and this is true,
Schade Island.

Have mercy, Lord, on me, sang her girlfriend
on the rocks as she immersed the notebooks
of STC into print on a screened-in porch.

He's just offshore, casting
an eye over the untroubled water
on all those improving the common law,
where nothing goes on
occurring to him
with a kind of largesse.

*

My mind continued composing its account at night,
I could hear it tracing glyphs on the hard substance

abundant in these waters
just off the aft deck to the tune of a gang of mosquitoes.

I could hear its running indifference to the indifference
of its medium,

and I couldn't help it,
I mean there was literally nothing I could do

to help, only listen to its business of joining words
with the tip of its thought on the ongoing granite.

*

Scarcely one in a hundred of these islands is capable of cultivation,
wrote a sincere and self-
divided advocate
for the First Nations
circa 1850, Peter Jones his very
white name, therefore in their present rude and wild magnificence
they must remain, till all nature
be put to confusion, and the elements melt away with fervent heat.

Precisely what might then become of them
he hardly needed to explain.
Perhaps a single undulating island
without, perhaps, the need of a name.

*

Gotham Island Wawasekona Island Omar Island Wall Island Doll Island Carlotta Island Qui-Vive Island Double Island Palestine Island Perdue Island Forage Island Sugar Island Iowa Island Jumbo Island Hardie Island Howl Island Echo Island Spectacle Island Ajax Island Turning Island Schade Island Skunk Island Big Bobs Island

*

Imagine him saying if
his father's form and meaning
merged
he'd make stones capable.
Was that likewise provocation
on his part, implying
stones were stones, alas,
the ghost
as composition
had its flaws?
You see he likes to cull
and crack assertions
from all over—No woman
no cry, and so on.

*

Procedural:
the natural law that moves
in everything will share
with loyal viewers
hard-won truths,
for instance this unusual situation:
just then it didn't occur to me
to be amazed but only later—
the pine can build its form of change
out from a single crevice
in a stone—
later at a moment when
I was susceptible to the consolations
of analogy.

*

Quartz unassimilated
in granite

preserves its own conception
of ore

obtained from a Polish quarry
as *twardy*

Mr. D's acquaintance with
the fact

expressed at the conclusion
of hard talks

eyes shut he hums, the first cut
is the deepest

*

The question was for many weeks should Mr. D
do something.

If only he did something, then time would gather
around him.

So long in coming, the answer in the end was
the questioning,

the current running one way under the wheelhouse
on this theme,

is the filament generating what there is
of anyone.

Say so and he'd laugh you off the island.
That's something.

*

Red and black
the lake behind the eyelids
where the thought that it's better
to do nothing lives.

*

No flocks to batten
he runs his eyes
over the page,
expert witness Dr. Bloom
unsloshing pebbles of his feel for the episode,
the book fished from her purse the minute
she went in, he must just stop it
with these undergrads.
Waiting in the waiting room,
he's paying.
If he's aware
of how she really feels,
which he is, it's a delicate thing
renouncing every drop of conceit in re his tactful way of knowing.

      *

At lunch he dives.
By way of aperitif he dives.
He dives for breakfast.

When you dive
the world pours up around you
continuously,

a ribbon of motion
defying end in
a tone that borders on arrogance.

Sounds and colors deepen
on their way to achieving
darkness and silence,
which keep receding.

A different situation however if
the entire time the thing
he was diving to reach
were diving just behind him.

*

With so elementary a thing as what I thought
I wouldn't venture burdening
the summer clouds

He hadn't had the time to bank a discipline
up from its root that some attain
just holding out

The undertaking seemed to me prodigious
in simplicity, to reckon and
then tell you what

How glutted with experience the rain must be
leaping off the clouds with one
trajectory

Deponent a rococo archipelago,
installer of the loopholes in
his line of thought

*

He reads such books
as are available about the rocks

A consequent significance
does not betray itself

But let the fallacy of place
live out its lease

"You can't create a landscape"
well, you can—

Rupert Brooke not far from here
revealed his education,

I have a perpetual feeling
a lake ought not to be this size.

*

Samuel de
Champlain drew
circles in lieu
of islands:
pebbles.

Runes littering
an inland sea, had they had
a voice might hymn,
so roundly having been
tucked away.

*

Soliloquy
—*alone place*—
conscripted into
patented theatricals
of the island empire only
decades after Hamlet, Lear, et
al. were first assembled into words,
what the playwright did in his time to flag
soliloquy was this: *Exeunt,* so every character not
intended to pause now and confide in me
generations later had to just get off
the stage. Ships were rushing out
from Amsterdam, Palos, Saint-
Malo, Bristol. Cooperation-
wise I'd say the age
was golden.

*

Sufficiently hidden in the side of this blue planet
I watched the moon take its time

levitating through the black windshield brushes
of pine at the edge of the island

till it worked its way into the smooth dark atmosphere above,
accelerating then and exposing in its wake

a twist of veins and ligaments swollen massive, jungle trailing
down to me, myself, stretching stretching stretching past endurance

*

All the girls are lovely by the seaside
all the girls are lovely by the sea:
among the cottages

one or two eccentrics
collect wax cylinders,

which in their day made such a potent rival
to the vinyl disc because—although listening
itself destroyed the one expressive continuous rille—

the cylinder could be shaved of sound
at home, made new anew

provided you knew the proper way to handle it, fingers
signaling victory or peace depending on the year
inside the tube

before carving it smooth: then it's capable
of bottling this, that is to say it's helpless to refuse.

                    *

The feeling possessing a man driving a fast car

(a woman can enjoy it also but the way
a tourist sips grappa in Treviso:
the burning down the throat's inseparable
from holiday
from what you really are)

has no exact correlative aboard a boat,
even on a boat that's very fast.

The water forms a fact
of greater power.

Like a female in a tight skirt,
it is
a fact.

*

Within the unflagging wringing concentration
that even a dippy vessel wants
in these waters

waits a state of mind not so much passionate
and cold in its stamina

as synced with the inefficiencies of time,
fused down into its crevices of scale,
happy in its specificities
that blanch when lifted from their element,
clustering atomic when a rock looms up
pink and nonnegotiable, and then

recorded on preexisting grooves in these islands
the pulsing air of the unsayable

would maybe sense
how certain belated sounds busy
themselves restitching its abolished movements.

*

He likes to circle phrases in the paper.
No one past one hundred thousand miles was such
assimilation, lifted from the news.

At times he circles sentences entire,
once or twice entire story. Do this
consistently enough, there comes a shining day

he fails to persuade himself the paper as a whole
does not deserve to be circled,
contained inside a solemn fat black border

around its fine serrated edges,
pledged to the icebox for ceremonies
whose scenery bit by bit's still on its way.

*

Here in the land Romanticism neglected
the Enlightenment passed by and planted
a shrub, a flag to flap and fling
the moon's weather, should you
wish it confirmed.

*

Second of all the French
then English, after the English
unseated the French and retreated from the English
then German weekenders and then
their rental cabins
named Winnetou, Apache, and (riveted
to the tallest pink slab)
Old Shatterhand.

Precisely which islands
were favored for summering
by the Wendat up from scorching Ontario
annually before 1623
is a matter of intense reenactment for children
not yet specialized in the relevant arts.

*

Not lakes but islands.

    Not islands but circulars.

      Not circulars but those very small achievements
that persuade us we are insulated from circumstance.

    Not circumstance but family chronicles

        shedding item by item their particulars
like desirable women stepping out of their clothes.

    Not their clothes but their parliaments.

      Not parliaments but a national literature.
Not land surveyors but aeons.

    Not aeons but islands.

      And not lakes.

    *

Either the outboard takes you
along a screen of rocks

disclosing the local
Hole in the Wall—
a channel manifesting

when the prow's near enough
to scrape mineral,
sides tall enough to make
kids cannonball—

at head of which he waits, a wanderer
above the sea of fog; or else

it's you on the promontory,
knee bent, scouting
his arrival in the dinghy,

his passage through the strait
cautious, as through a condensed
atmospheric aesthetics, the style
imposed by years or rocks.

*

As if the moon some
three thousand million summers ago
was bored and thought
to key the earth

just where the paint job
was most excessive,
material and
potential both

As if the sun said, fine
break it you buy it
or words to that effect

*

What rock and water share
(astonishment to others
not themselves)

reflected Mr. D—
indifferent
Linnaean in his time—

contrary to earth is
immunity (sublime)
to our ongoing

performances.
Should some international
undocumented

wish to pursue
a lifestyle entirely free
from applause,

he reflected, this
would be the place.
He glances round.

*

As water
levels drop
and drop,
two islands
will become
one.

A tidally locked body
takes just as long
to rotate around its
own axis as it
does to revolve around
its partner.

Because the moon's mass is a considerable fraction
of the earth's, it exerts a gravitational force
on oceans as it orbits overhead, producing the
tides, or put another way, you can stand
on shore twice daily and witness the very
water flinging itself upwards.

*

For him the stand
of pines abruptly shifts
as one

from island to island:

the galley's
open window
pivoting in a breeze

*

The pines absorb the night, its themes and fabrics,
a lowering of blinds within blinds and glances perceiving glances,

till nothing of night remains in the air and the sky begins to demonstrate
again its essential property of flaring from all quarters

and all morning the pines sparely with a kind of jealous, pointed
attention unleash their reserves, granting each hour

before noon its cool underpinning and each pine
the work of expressing its individual silence

Some of these poems were previously published in the following journals, to whose editors grateful acknowledgment is made: *The New Yorker, The Paris Review,* the *London Review of Books, Harper's, The New York Review of Books, The Nation, The Baffler,* and the *Literary Review of Canada.*

Thanks also to the generous support of Yaddo, where some of these poems were written.

"The Tempest": the penultimate stanza is taken from Michel de Montaigne's essay "Of Diverting or Diversion" in *Shakespeare's Montaigne: The Florio Translation of the Essays.*

"Thirty Thousand Islands"

"This, we thought, his country": stanza 2 is drawn (slightly altered) from James Joyce's *Portrait of the Artist as a Young Man.*

"Somewhere nearby": the words "azoic rock,/hornblende granite" are taken from Lorine Niedecker's *Lake Superior.* Details in the third and fourth stanzas can be traced to Kathleen Coburn's *In Pursuit of Coleridge.*

"Within the unflagging wringing concentration": the words "the pulsing air of the unsayable" are drawn, slightly altered, from Stanley Cavell's *The World Viewed: Reflections on the Ontology of Film.*

"As water": the second stanza is taken from the Wikipedia entry for "tidal locking."